Dedication

Mark, my high school sweetheart, my husband, the love of my life, and the only person I want to grow older with. Thank you for believing in me, supporting every venture, and for loving me in spite of all of my flaws. I love you, and am grateful for every single day I am able to share with you.

Damon, Autumn and Alyssa, my amazing children, I couldn't be more proud of you. You are all beautiful, intelligent, with fabulous personalities, and I am excited to watch you grow, learn, and find your own passions! I love you dearly.

Mary Aranowski, thank you for having such a generous heart. I'm in awe every time I'm with you. Thank you for loving my entire family, thank you for holding me tight when I thought I was falling, and thank you for standing by my side through every victory. I love you!

Mark & Sharon Hoelscher, thank you for believing in me, and my vision. Your encouragement and support is astounding to me, and I will always be incredibly appreciative.

Jonell Kehias, thank you for propelling me to this amazing place in my life. Your friendship, combined with a willingness to continually brainstorm, help divert crises, laugh and cry with me, is an amazing blessing. Thank you.

Mom and Dad, I miss you both terribly, with an immense sadness I didn't know existed. Each time I look at my children, I pray I get it at least a little right. I know if I parent even a tiny bit as well as you both did, my children will have it made. I love you both, and I'm so sorry you aren't physically with me to enjoy this achievement. But, in spirit you always are, and I am grateful for your continued guidance.

Using Coupons:

Encouraging Hope

An Inspirational
How-To Book on
Utilizing Coupons
for the Greater Good

Kimberly McCormick

Using Coupons: Encouraging Hope

Copyright © 2011 by Kimberly McCormick

ISBN 978-0-9724027-2-9

Table of Contents

Foreword

A little over a year ago I opened a window. And in flew Kimberly McCormick. That's how it works sometimes, if you're lucky.

I am in charge of increasing and retaining readers at The Pantagraph, a mid-size newspaper located in Bloomington, Illinois. With the explosion of web sites, news channels and magazines vying for the limited time of people, I knew I had to exploit one of the great assets of the newspaper.

Coupons.

We had been running a column by a nationally syndicated coupon columnist. It was ok. I never received any feedback from readers, and the information was generic.

My boss and I began kicking around the idea that if we could get someone local, someone who could really promote the value of OUR coupons and show readers how to maximize the savings, then we'd be onto something.

I began and ended my research with my own newspaper. A few years back we had done an article on Kim. From the article, I realized she knew how to save a buck. But, I needed so much more than that. I needed someone who could write, and write well. I needed someone who could come up with a new angle on couponing each and every week. I needed someone who could meet deadlines. I needed someone who could resonate with our readers. I needed … Kim. Of course, I didn't know at the time that it WAS Kim that I needed.

I called Kim at 9:05 on a Tuesday morning. She was at my office at 10:30. Kim was in nice jeans and a grey zippered Disney sweatshirt on a cold central Illinois day. "Do you like my winter coat?" she asked. "I'd rather spend my money on clothes for my kids than buy a winter coat." And that pretty much sums Kim up.

So we talked. Actually, she talked and I listened. She started speaking a foreign language of hang tags and Catalinas. I was blown away with her couponing knowledge, her wheeling and dealing, her stories of buying pudding which allowed her to purchase children's items, all of which she donated. It was obvious Kim knew about couponing. What I didn't know was if she could communicate that to our readers, and if our readers would care.

Short answer: yes and yes. Kim's writing talent was evident from the sample column she submitted. Writing was a gift she inherited from her poet father. Kim had always offered seminars, but now she had to double the number she offered. She moved out of her home office and into a retail office. She is the most popular presenter at our community Money Smart Week. She gives easy-to-follow, concrete advice on how to turn coupons into savings. And she does it all with a mission in mind. Kim is the founder of Retire with Coupons, Inc. Its mission is "Using Coupons: Encouraging Hope."

She teaches people from all walks of life how to save big money with coupons. This isn't extreme couponing. It's not hoarding or cheating the system. It's simply maximizing the savings manufacturers and stores offer.

And if you need that money to support your family, that's great because you will have extra cash to pay other bills or to enjoy life a little more. But if you're doing ok, if perhaps you don't need three toothbrushes, then donate the extras to soldiers overseas, to a food bank, or to a domestic violence shelter. Use coupons to make someone else's life better.

By purchasing this book you've just opened a window of your own. It's a quick read. Simple and straightforward. Just like Kim. And with a whole lot of heart.

Read on and save. And encourage hope. One coupon at a time.

Jonell Kehias
Marketing/Retention Manager
The Pantagraph

I am who I am

The first words always seem to be the hardest. Where do I begin? How do I start the process of sharing my life, my ideals, and my mission? I've sat here staring at a blank sheet of paper for weeks, and decided, finally, to just dive in – to let my personality be my guide, and allow my friends, family, and fans appreciate who I am, and what I stand for.

Although I'm often recognized as "the coupon lady" or "the one in the newspaper," I'm a mom before I'm anything else. I have three children. Damon is nine, Autumn is eight, and Alyssa just turned five. My kids drive me crazy with the incessant fighting, arguing over where someone is going to sit, and then whining about how life isn't fair. But it is these three precious beings that push me forward, allow me to marvel in the firsts of everything, and realize with each passing day how to love with a fierceness I can't even begin to describe.

I am also a wife, married to Mark, who was my high school sweetheart, and still remains my best friend. I am a volunteer, and I coordinate donations for other organizations. I am the founder of two non-profits, I served on the board of directors for another non-profit, and I am consistently involved with fundraising committees to raise awareness of domestic violence. I also spend a tremendous amount of time assisting at my children's school, and I've served as vice president, and president, of their school PTO.

I am a weekly columnist for The Pantagraph in Bloomington, Illinois, as well as a workshop facilitator for my own company,

Retire With Coupons, Inc.   Our mission is Using Coupons: Encouraging Hope, but my entire life has been spent being mission oriented, helping others when I could, and if I couldn't do it alone, spearheading projects to involve others to offer hope and help up to those in need.

I'm Kimberly McCormick.   I'm a mom, wife, entrepreneur, writer, speaker, volunteer, and advocate.   I'm blessed, and grateful, every single moment of every single day.

Highlights for Children

When I was thirteen years old, I wrote a letter to the editor of Highlights for Children. My letter was published, and the editor sent the following letter to my home:

October 12, 1988

Dear Kim:

Thank you for writing to HIGHLIGHTS. You wrote that you want to help the hungry, the homeless, and others, but you don't have the money they ask for on television.

Kim, donating money is only one way to help people. You might help by becoming a volunteer at a local hospital, nursing home, day care center, or a charity dealing with the homeless. You might write an editorial for the school paper or give a presentation in class that will help others become aware that people are in need of help. You are helping even by talking to friends about the problems of the homeless and the hungry, because you are making your friends aware of those problems.

I think it's terrific that you're concerned about people, and I'm glad you're one of our readers. Best wishes to you from all of us at HIGHLIGHTS.

Sincerely,

Kent L. Brown, Jr.
Editor

I was thrilled then to receive such a great letter, with promising suggestions of how to help others. And, I'm proud to say I have done all of these, and continue to do so, as we raise awareness, find solutions, and work towards helping our community as a whole!

Summer Time Savings

I first began using coupons during the summer of 1993. I was a freshman in college, and had my very first apartment! There were a lot of bills, and they were much more expensive than I was anticipating. While looking through Sunday newspaper inserts, I found an advertisement for a coupon organizer, and was then introduced to a coupon magazine! There was a learning curve, but for each deal I participated in, I became better and better at saving money!

For example, Jewel-Osco featured a new chewable Tylenol tab called Tylenol ToGo. They were on sale for $1, and the same week the sale was effective, a $1 coupon appeared in the Sunday coupon insert making the product free!

Target offers store coupons, which can be combined with manufacturer coupons. By utilizing sale prices, I purchased two boxes of fruit roll ups, 16 small cereal cups, four packages of Huggies travel wipes, one bag of goldfish crackers, three toothbrushes, and four packages of airhead candy. My total, after all of my coupons, was only 41¢!

Over time, and as a new homeowner, I wanted a new stove – the new and exciting flat top stove! I wouldn't settle for anything else. Sears offered zero percent financing for a full year, so by dividing up my entire purchase over twelve months, I knew how much I needed monthly to pay it in full without any penalties. By using all of my coupon savings, I was able to make my monthly payments, and actually had it paid off before my year was over.

As I became comfortable matching sales with coupons, while learning and understanding coupon policies and legalities, I knew I could take this hobby and make it into something that had a true purpose!

What's in a Name?

In 2001, I was intrigued by a statistic that showed an annual amount being saved, compounded at some ridiculous rate, could actually be worth a million dollars by retirement!

Now, ten years later, I've learned that earning a million dollars for retirement by investing my coupon savings may be a bit extreme, but the amount of savings is truly nothing to chuckle at!

The national standards for the purchase of food, based on an IRS guideline*, for a family of four, is $752 a month! This means, on average, a family of four is spending this amount for food only! This doesn't include cleaning supplies, health and beauty items, diapers, or even pet supplies!

Let's assume, with the help of our company, we can take that $752 and make it $400. You've now just saved $352 a month. If we invest this amount of $4224 in a savings account with a 1.5% rate, and let it grow for just five years, you'll have $21,917.96.**

That's a lot of money!

So, although we won't be retiring with our coupon savings, it's certainly a hefty amount that may be put towards retirement! And, if you choose not to hang on to it for the long term, becoming debt free, providing financial assistance to loved ones, and giving you peace of mind certainly makes this "hobby" a very wise investment, indeed!

Using that insight in 2001, I came up with the name Retire With Coupons, and registered our website domain that we still use today!

*http://www.irs.gov/businesses/small/article/0,,id=104627,00.html
**http://www.moneychimp.com/calculator/compound_interest_calculator.htm

Retire With Coupons, Inc.

Now, 18 years after I began college, I'm still using coupons, and I'm sharing my knowledge and experiences with others. In November, 2009, Retire With Coupons went from being just a website with tidbits of information on couponing to a full fledged mission oriented company!

In March of 2010, I was blessed with an opportunity to be a weekly columnist for The Pantagraph in Bloomington, Illinois, and our unique vision became more quickly recognized and individuals began to understand the importance of our mission!

Retire With Coupons, Inc. wants to give back in the truest form by going full circle. We provide educational workshops with essential information to families on budgeting in an extraordinary way. Our events focus on the use of coupons, and how to stretch budgets within an individual and/or family's means. It covers the basics of coupon use, including where to find coupons, organizational information, finding current sales, store promotions, local store policies and legalities, and of course, specific, detailed explanations of some of my best deals!

"Once you choose hope, anything's possible."
Christopher Reeve

Our Promise to Our Community

With every workshop held at our office, we do our best to uphold inexpensive registration fees while requesting attendees bring items we distribute to organizations within our community!

We are proud to support numerous organizations in our area, and are honored to hear donations are being made, after our events, by individuals who took our information to heart, and are using it to better lives!

With every donation made, we sort by specific needs and donate between Clare House, a local food pantry, Neville House, our only domestic violence shelter in our county, and Promise Council which works to eliminate barriers to education for elementary students, as well as their families.

We also collect small stuffed animals, toys, books, coloring books, as well as art supplies, including, but not limited to: crayons, markers, and colored pencils.

The stuffed animals, toys, and books are donated to our local Community Cancer Center in honor of my dad who died from pancreatic cancer. I pledged the treasure chest would never be empty, and it is our goal to always have enough for every child that walks into this amazing organization.

The art supplies are donated to local elementary schools in honor of my mama. She was an amazing artist, and we want to provide as much as we can to students who may not be able to afford all of the requested school supplies, as well as assist teachers in their quest to encourage creativity.

March 15, 2011

Dear Kimberly McCormick,

On behalf of the CDV team, we would like to thank your company, Retire With Coupons, for your generous donations to the Neville House. The packs of pudding for groups, the non-perishable food items for us to use for hotel stay families and the paper goods supplies have been more definitely helpful and useful to our clients. Thank you for your generosity and continued support in helping families up and out of domestic violence.

Sincerely,

Senna Adjabeng, MS, ICDVP
CDV Program Manager

May 6, 2011

Dear Kimberly,

I wanted to take a quick moment to thank you so much for all you have done to assist our families at Pepper Ridge. The hygiene supplies you are able to gather for us have been greatly appreciated. Every family I have a home visit with, I am able to provide them with the supplies you have passed on to our school and they are grateful for all the items. You have been instrumental in supplying a much needed request I have of families. With the increasing costs of supplies, food, gas, etc., the need is growing ever so much. I personally thank you, because you have helped me in being able to offer these much needed items to families whom are trying to do the best they can to make ends meet.

Again, thank you so much for all your efforts and supports in making a different for the families at Pepper Ridge.

Respectfully,

Kim Page
School Social Worker
Unit 5, Pepper Ridge Elementary

June 14, 2011

Dear Kimberly:

Your support helps the Community Cancer Center make a difference in cancer care.

Please accept our sincere appreciation and thanks for your ongoing contributions to the Children's Treasure Chest. Picking an article from the Treasure Chest is a highlight for the children who come into the Community Cancer Center – whether they are attending a support group or waiting with a loved one. When they pull a game or toy from the chest it helps them feel more at home and less afraid. The Community Cancer Center Foundation is indeed fortunate to have supporters like you. Your generosity enables us to change lives for the better through our programs and services.

Thank you again for your commitment to our organization.

Sincerely,

Barbara J. Nathan, FAAMA
Executive Director

BJN/jm

"To give hope to someone occurs when you teach them how to use the tools to do it for themselves."

Byron Pulsifer

Our Services & Products

We offer our monthly subscription service to help families duplicate good deals allowing them to keep more cash in their pocket for other items they may need, but couldn't previously afford. Our Shopping Crew provides shopping lists for eight different stores. These lists detail information about local sales, and the coupons that match the sales. We also include information on store promotions, such as Catalina coupons and extra care bucks, and when possible, links to online printable coupons.

A weekly recipe is often included in our shopping crew, once a week, based on ingredients you'll find in our weekly shopping lists. This allows you to take good deals and turn them into amazing meals!

We offer assistance on finding coupon sources, as well as social gatherings where everyone is encouraged to swap extra coupons, donate items to local organizations, and become a part of something bigger than ourselves!

Individuals and businesses have stepped up to offer funds for individuals to take our workshops and subscribe to our monthly shopping crew that may not be able to afford it otherwise, and Retire With Coupons focuses on donating items needed directly to local organizations! Amazing, huh?!

"I am enjoying the subscription to the Shopping Crew and find it helpful the way you break it down by store and then list the items that are available at the best price at that particular store. I find myself looking forward to getting the Shopping Crew twice a week and have found it makes my shopping excursions a lot easier knowing what stores I want to shop at and the prices of the items I can get for the best value."
Ginny S.

"Since participating in the Retire With Coupons workshop, my grocery bills have been cut in half. My family has been able to expand the variety of food we eat, and we never go shopping without a list! My daughters are learning from an early age that we really can make a budget and stick to it! Now I recommend Retire With Coupons to everyone!
Vikki B.

"Retire With Coupons Rocks!"
Damon M.
(Kimberly's son ☺)

Our product line is a three tiered system designed to really organize all coupons, and allow each individual to feel completely in control of their savings. These products allow each person to utilize my system as I do, which will help eliminate frustration and confusion, and allow every individual to start saving money immediately!

Our first resource is our File Tote Organizer. I don't cut my coupons. I file them all by full insert labeled by date, insert (Red Plum, Proctor & Gamble, General Mills, Unilever, or Smart Source) and newspaper. I recycle all of my coupons after approximately four months, and I utilize an excel database to find exactly what coupon I'm searching for.

If you file coupons by full insert, you need to know where to find what you're looking for. Our excel database provides you a formatted list every week with coupons we've received locally! This allows you to use the "edit, find" feature to find exactly where your needed coupons are! Each coupon description tells you the date they were printed, which insert to find them in, as well as what newspaper they were in!

Because there are always loose coupons, our next product is our Categorized Organizer. This flip top organizer includes our top 20 categories to assist your organization. These coupons may be coupons you've cut, coupons you've found at stores or coupons your friends and family members have given to you. This organizer keeps all of your coupons in one place so you may find them when you need them.

My absolute favorite organizer is our Store Organizer! I

recommend this organizer if you aren't certain which product you want to begin with! My organizer includes headings for all the local stores I shop at, but can be customized based on your location or favorite stores. When you have your planned grocery list, and you've cut your coupons, put them both in the respective store pocket. By labeling each pocket by store name, you allow yourself to be as organized as possible before you reach the grocery store!

For more details on my organizational approach, please visit our corporate site at http://www.retirewithcoupons.com/.

Commit to Savings

Lesson #1: What are you currently spending?

The first thing you need to do is determine what you're currently spending on items you bring home to consume. This includes food, health and beauty items, cleaning supplies, as well as baby and pet items. If you consistently purchase for individuals who don't live in your home, please include this amount in your budget. However, dining out, including drive thru, should not be included in this amount.

When you have a beginning amount, it's much easier to work towards a specific goal! And, when you know your starting number, and what you want the end result to be, you will find yourself more excited and more motivated in making these lifestyle changes!

Lesson #2: What do you need your household budget to be?

The next thing you need to know is what your end result should be. If you're spending $1,000 a month now, where do you need to be? Would you be happy at $800, or based on other expenses, would saving $500 a month create amazing opportunities for you?

Please think long and hard about this. Don't just come up with a number that sounds good. Please look at your expenses, and determine what you need on a monthly basis to survive. Once you know what has to be paid versus your income, setting a household budget will be easier.

Lesson #3: How committed are you?

Please understand right now this is nothing like the 'extreme couponing' you see depicted on television. Our mission is to assist you, to create a means to save money, and to ensure you have what you need if there's a crisis. I am not going to share with you how to get 1,000 candy bars free just because. I will share with you how to buy multiple items, at a lower cost, to allow you some freedom from worry. I will explain how I've bought hundreds of items, very inexpensively, specifically to donate, in the hopes you will take these educational tips to provide for others, too.

So, how committed are you? Are you excited enough to do this for the rest of your life? Are you ready to shop like I do on a regular basis, allowing for the ups and downs of the sales cycle, being ready for the next big deal, and being open to buying to donate? Or, are you kind of excited, but only short term? Is there a bill you need to pay, or a vacation you'd like to go on? Are you using coupons as your vehicle to reach those goals? Or, are you comfortable with your budget, but you want to buy specifically to give back to others without increasing what you're spending?

Once you figure out where you are in the levels of commitment, and you've determined your starting budget and your end goals, utilizing coupons will open up an entirely new world for you!

"I've been involved with Retire With Coupons for about 4 months now. My average grocery bill for my family of four was around $800-$900 a month. Through the help of Retire With Coupons workshops, I've been able to cut my grocery bill in half. It's so exciting to see the extra money in our monthly budget. We have cut down tremendously on using our credit card and feel a sense of relief knowing we are making ends meet and not going down the road of debt anymore. My husband has recently had his job hours cut, but I know we will be fine due to the fellowship and direction given to me by being part of the Retire With Coupons crew. This is truly a one of a kind organization, and I am blessed to be a part of it. I am looking forward to the day when my family can give back more than what we are doing now."

Jodi C.

"Hope is faith holding out its hand in the dark."
George Iles

Inventory Everything

My hope is you've now taken a close look at your beginning budget, where you want to be, and how committed you are to making the changes to reach your goal!

You're now ready for the next step!

<u>Lesson #4: What do you currently have to utilize at home?</u>

Take inventory of what you have in your kitchen, pantry, cabinets, and any storage areas! If you have items at home you can utilize, it is less money you need to spend out of pocket immediately.

Do you have rice? Pasta? Spices? Do you have meat in the freezer hidden by something else? This is the best time to take a good look at everything you have, check for expiration dates, and determine if the items will be used.

Please also inventory non-food items. How much toilet paper do you have? Paper towels or napkins? Do you have laundry soap, toothpaste, and toothbrushes?

<u>Lesson #5: Document Everything!</u>

Once you've inventoried everything in your home, if something is expired, please throw it away. If it's current, but you know no one will use it, put it in a box to donate it!

After you've tossed and donated, write everything else down, so you have a record of what you have!

After you know what you have, decide what items you may need to purchase to create entire meals. Any items that are "leftover" will then be the center of your future meals. Your first shopping list becomes the ingredients you need to purchase to utilize the items already at home.

Were you surprised at how many items you had tucked away in your home? Are you able to utilize most of it for meals? Did you find non-food items tucked away, but forgotten? If so, you are already saving money by being creative with what you have!

Sales Cycle

It's now time to take a look at a bigger picture.

What do you use over a six to eight week period of time? How much hamburger do you cook? Chicken? Pasta? How much toothpaste do you use, and how many loads of laundry do you complete? How many rolls of papers towels do you go through, and how much milk and cereal do your kids eat?

Lesson #6: How much do you use during a sales cycle?

Take a typical week in your household and write down everything you use. I realize no one ever has typical weeks, but take the most normal week you can, and jot down everything from the amount of milk you drink to how many bags of chips you ate to how much toilet paper was used. Then, multiple each number by six or eight. These are your magic numbers!

Lesson #7: How much do you use during a sales cycle?

By now you've determined your monthly spending, your commitment level, what you'd like your household budget to actually be, what you already have at home, and what you use in a six to eight week time frame.

The six to eight weeks is important. It's our typical sales cycle. If you buy something today on sale, it's likely it will be on sale for the same as, or less than, what you paid in approximately six to eight weeks.

If you can buy enough, during a good sale, to last you six to eight weeks, you will save tremendously because you aren't buying at the store's pricing discretion!

Now what?

It's time to compare the "leftovers" of what you have at home with your six to eight week list. Remember, the "leftovers" are items you have at home, but you don't have everything you need to create a meal.

If your list shows you have three boxes of pasta, but no pasta sauce, you then look at your six to eight week list and determine how much spaghetti you eat in that amount of time.

If your family has pasta night once a week, you need to purchase enough for those six meals. At this time, assuming you only need one box of pasta and one jar of sauce, your shopping list would consist of three boxes of pasta and six jars of sauce. That would be enough to carry you through for the next six weeks.

By doing this for every item on your six to eight week list, you'll know your shopping target. And, when a great sale comes along, you know how many you need to buy before the next sale arrives!

And, when you wrote down what you already had at home, you immediately saved yourself from buying more than you currently need from the present sales cycle!

Let's Shop

Now, you should be ready to shop. You have your six to eight week list of items you use regularly, and you know what you have at home to begin with. But, there's one more thing to consider!

Lesson #8: Are you brand loyal to everything?

The more brand loyal you are, the harder it will be to save money effectively. It's absolutely fine, however, to have a few items you love, and aren't willing to give up.

Pepsi is my favorite drink, and I always tell people I'll be the person paying $10 per two liter because it's the one thing I refuse to change. It is what it is! But, if you're brand loyal to everything, you won't have the opportunity to save with each sales cycle.

If you're willing to try new things, experiment with different recipes, and look for comparable items, you'll do very well using coupons. The more flexible you are, the sooner you'll see the decrease in the amount of money you're spending.

As an example, Dole and Del Monte both had canned fruit on sale for $1 each. There were no coupons for Del Monte, but there was a coupon for 50¢ on two Dole products! By buying Dole, and using the coupon at a store that doubled the value, you've instantly saved 50%! Because both Dole and Del Monte are similar in quality, taste, and price, using the available coupon helps drastically decrease the amount of money you have to spend!

Don't Buy Just Anything!

One of the biggest mistakes individuals make when beginning to use coupons is buying items just because they have a coupon. We get excited! We want savings immediately, so we jump on board and start buying everything we can with a coupon because we are now saving money! Right?

Lesson #9: Don't buy an item just because you have a coupon!

If you buy something because you have a coupon, but have no intention of using the product, or donating it, you've spent more money than you needed to.

If you have a coupon, and you use it on an item that is regular price, although you're saving money, you aren't saving as much as you could!

In order to truly see the benefit of using coupons to save money, you have to begin searching for items on sale, and see what coupons are available to use on that particular product. Instead of using a coupon just to use it, you'll be using coupons to take home items you'll benefit from, without breaking the bank! It's always best to combine a store sale with a coupon to lower your out of pocket costs.

If toothpaste is normally $3, and you use a $1 coupon, you're still saving $1. But, if you wait until the toothpaste is on sale for $2, and you use your coupon on the sale price, you're actually saving $2! You are immediately seeing a dramatic increase in savings!

"Believe deep down in your heart that you're destined to do great things."
Joe Paterno

There's Always an Exception

Lesson #10: There's always an exception to the rule!

Our mission is Using Coupons: Encouraging Hope. It is our belief when individuals learn how to use coupons effectively, they will begin to see a greater purpose.

Once you have reached your budget goals, it is my hope you will take the knowledge you've learned and use it to better your community.

Although I mentioned previously you should never buy an item just because you have a coupon, there is an exception!

If you are able to purchase an item for very little, and you can afford to do so, please purchase items to donate.

This is the perfect opportunity to not only help yourself, your family, as well as your loved ones, but to also make someone else's life better!

"More that anything else, people will always remember you for how you made them feel."
Shadonna Richards, A Gift of Hope

The Proof is in the Pudding

Have you ever considered how coupons could change lives? This is my favorite story with an amazing purpose! It's the first large scale deal I did, and it was also the first deal that showed me how using coupons could change lives!

Hunt's pudding and Toys R Us had an incredible co-op together. On the inside of each specially marked four serving package of pudding, there was a certificate to use at Toys R Us! You'd scratch off the amount, and you were promised at least $1. You'd then turn in the certificates for Geoffrey dollars to use on any products within their store!

The pudding was on sale for $1.19, and in the Toys R Us monthly advertisement, there was a coupon for Hunt's pudding for 40¢. The store that had the pudding in stock doubled the value of each coupon taking off 80¢ on each package I purchased! By utilizing the coupon, my cost became only 39¢, but I was still earning at least $1 to use at Toys R Us!

Although 39¢ for a four pack of pudding is a great deal, it got better! The store carrying the pudding began tripling the coupon value! So, now my 40¢ coupon is worth $1.19 (the coupon value will never exceed the purchase price of an item) making my pudding absolutely free, but I was still earning at least $1 to use at Toys R Us!

At this point, I wanted to see how big of a deal I could make this into! I asked the store director if he'd special order the pudding, so I didn't clear any shelves, and I asked the manager of Toys R

Us if he had extra monthly sales ads I could have for the coupons. The store director agreed to special order the pudding, and as luck would have it, it was the last day of the month, so the manager at Toys R Us agreed to give me extra ads. At this point, I would have taken any amount, but the manager went above and beyond, and gave me every single ad he could find. He even pulled them out of trash cans for me!

Can you see the potential? After cutting out every coupon I was given, and purchasing every four pack of pudding I had requested, I purchased over 500 packages of pudding!

My out of pocket cost, however, was closer to $65, and I received over $500 to use at Toys R Us! WOW! Now do you see how big this could be?!

Fortunately, this particular pudding didn't need to be refrigerated, and a majority was donated to a local non-profit organization. I then used the $500 in Geoffrey dollars to buy for 40 children for the Angel Tree program that Christmas!

This is thinking outside of the box. This is changing the way we shop! This is changing lives! This is Using Coupons: Encouraging Hope!

$150 Monthly Challenge

In January of 2009, I challenged myself to spend only $150 a month on everything my family needed, including all of our meats, dairy, produce, health and beauty, and pet supplies. This amount also had to encompass baby supplies, including diapers for our youngest daughter!

It was incredibly difficult for me! Every trip had to be to diligently planned, and every item I needed had to have a coupon, or I had to find a way to buy something else to get something less expensive. It was an amazing journey, and I learned a lot! But, I also learned it's not a challenge I wanted to repeat! ☺

These were my monthly totals:

January	$175.01
February	$197.67
March	$207.96
April	$190.35
May	$188.11
June	$137.79

During the months I spent more, there were more deals I could stockpile for future use. March was my most expensive month, but I also brought home more items than any other month.

June was my least expensive month, but typically you find more deals to stockpile during an academic school year. There are ups and downs to each sales period, and I find more deals consistently, that allow me to bring home more in quantity, between August and May.

My average for the six months of this challenge was $182.82 a month! For a family of five, a dog and a cat, it's a pretty good household budget! But, more typically for me, is my average budget of approximately $250 a month!

Here are some of my deals during these six months!

#1 Transaction

Donuts (for the kids, of course!)
8 Packages of Healthy Ones Lunch Meat

The donuts were $1, and the lunch meat was on sale for $1 each. I had eight 75¢ coupons for the lunch meat, so it was only a quarter per package -- a great deal for lunches! My total out of pocket was $3.09.

#2 Transaction

1 Culinary Circle pizza
1 package Jewel brand shredded cheese
1 package Tortillas
1 box Macaroni & Cheese
1 container Blueberries
1 container Raspberries
1 bag of Oranges
2.43# of Bananas
2 bags of Fresh Express Salad

I used a $3 coupon for the pizza, five $2 coupons off produce, $1.50 on bananas when you buy two salads, and coupon for the macaroni & cheese. My total was only $2.92!

Transaction #3

I bought a deli platter on sale for $12.99. There was a coupon in the sales ad that stated I could get an eight piece bucket of chicken for free, if I bought the deli platter! Well, lucky for me, I had a $10 specialty coupon good on any deli platter! I paid $2.99 for the platter, got the chicken free, and then added on the two sides and rolls with the chicken for $3! My total cost for everything was only $6.37, and fed my family of five for two meals!

Transaction #4

Target allows you to stack a manufacturer coupon with their store coupons! I bought two six packs of Mott's Applesauce. I used two $1 off Target store coupons, and two 55¢ off manufacturer coupons! They were only $1.69 each, so my total out of pocket was just 29¢ for twelve servings!

Transaction #5

This transaction had so many items that I won't break it all down, but out of a total of 52 items purchased, I used 42 coupons! Between store promotions, and my coupons, I saved a total of $148.87! I paid a grand total of just $6.62, and $2.32 was tax!

This is my daughter, Alyssa, showcasing my receipt! She was two years old here, and the receipt was nearly as tall as she was!

Where are the Coupons?

The best place to find your coupons is your Sunday newspaper. Due to a lot of coupon fraud, retailers are more hesitant to accept internet printables, and although technology is progressing, not all stores are accepting digital coupons.

There are five inserts you want to watch for! The first two are SmartSource and Red Plum. There are also three additional inserts, all by manufacturer! These include Proctor & Gamble, Unilever, and General Mills.

In our workshops, I often share I'm rarely worried about finding extra coupons in the SmartSource or Red Plum because they are fairly interchangeable. For example, if you find a Campbell's soup coupon in one insert, you may find a Progresso soup coupon in another insert the following week. They have similar quality, taste, and price point. However, when Proctor & Gamble, Unilever, or General Mills have an insert, it's best to purchase multiple copies! Because these are specific to manufacturer, it's more difficult to get additional coupons, if you only received one original coupon.

Let's assume you receive a $1 off Tide coupon, but there's no great sale, so you opt not to get multiple inserts. But, two weeks later, there's a huge sale on Tide products, and you need multiple coupons to stockpile the item at a tremendous discount! Because you didn't purchase multiple inserts originally, it will be harder to find extras now, especially without incurring a much higher cost to purchase the individual needed coupon.

It's much better to have multiple full inserts, each week, than to try and buy or trade for the individual coupons you need when a sale begins! By knowing you have multiples of every insert, you know you can stockpile at a great price, bringing home more for less money!

How many coupon inserts do I need?

I always suggest having at least three sets of coupons to maximize your savings. Yes, this means buying three Sunday newspapers every week. Three is a great number if you're just beginning this amazing hobby. Three will allow you to get organized, find a system that works for you and your lifestyle, and you won't be overwhelmed as you learn your store's policies and legalities.

As you become more familiar with using coupons, and are comfortable with your organizational system, I suggest getting four, five or six copies weekly. I personally get ten copies delivered every week, and I often buy more if I need multiples for a deal to donate to a local organization!

Aside from the local papers, there are numerous internet sites which will allow you to print coupons! Our website, http://www.retirewithcoupons.com, has a printable coupon page for your use! All of the coupons are legitimate, and we earn approximately 1¢ per print which goes directly back into our mission of using coupons, and encouraging hope.

Contact manufacturers! Almost every company has a website. Use the contact form to send your comments, and tell them how much you enjoy their products! Ask to be added to their mailing lists, and ask specifically for coupons, special offers, or other promotional items they share with their customers! Most companies will do what they can to keep you as a customer, and they are happy to send you deals to entice you to buy more of their products!

Don't forget to ask your friends, family, and co-workers for their extra coupons. Ask them, please, to not cut out the coupons, but to keep them as intact as possible. By utilizing the hanging file organization system, you don't want to begin with loose coupons!

There are additional coupons, as well, often found within the stores.

Peelies are coupons found attached to products. They are to be utilized when you buy the product, and can be peeled off as you are checking out. Here's an example found on a box of cereal:

Tear Pads are coupons that can be literally torn off their pad. I often see these on freezer sections, as well as in snack aisles. This particular coupon was found near the popcorn!

Blinkies are machines that often have a timing mechanism. You pull one coupon out, and the second follows immediately. But, there is then a delay before the next coupon is available for you to take. Blinkies received their name from the red light that often blinks on top of each device! I often find these coupons near products in the refrigerated sections.

How Much Time Will This Take?

Although I am often asked how much time I spend shopping, I usually spend more time at the stores than the traditional shopper. This is my 9-5 job, and I'm blessed with the opportunity to shop to literally try deals to see what works! But, I also donate a lot, and that takes time, too!

The variations will depend on how many people you are shopping for, and how well your organizational system works for you. If you are shopping for two people versus ten, or you want to fill your food pantry, it will take more time. But, if your organizational system doesn't work for you, you will waste time trying to find lost coupons, being frustrated over expired coupons, or be flustered while trying to check out.

How long before I see the benefits?

In our workshops, I really emphasize how important it is to stick with couponing consistently for at least sixteen weeks. Sixteen weeks allows you to experience the six to eight week sales cycles twice, and it also allows you to become more comfortable with organization and store policies.

It's important to understand you will notice an increase in your stockpile before you notice a decrease in the amount of money you're spending. It's normal to spend the same amount for the first six to eight weeks as you build up your pantry. You will notice decreases, but the significant financial difference usually comes between 12 and 16 weeks.

"Spend time each day being grateful for all the things that are right and good in your life. "
Elaine St. James, 365 Simple Reminders

Feel Good Donations

Mentos sugarless gum was on sale for $1. There were 55¢ coupons in our local Sunday insert. One of our local stores doubles up to 50¢, and any value from 51¢ to 99¢ becomes equivalent to $1. This means all of my 55¢ coupons became $1, making each package of gum free!

I purchased 125 packs of gum, used 125 coupons gathered from friends and family, and spent only 69¢ in tax! I then donated a majority of the gum to my children's elementary school which was then used for literary and carnival prizes!

Below is a photograph of Healthy Choice soup. The cost? After the store's sale price, coupons, and a manufacturer offer, I paid only tax for all of this! It was all donated to a local food pantry!

This picture shows 116 boxes of cereal, and five boxes of fruit snacks I purchased for only $10.25! They were donated to our local Clare House! On another occasion, my family and I donated 72 boxes of cereal, and 24 boxes of granola bars, and paid less than $12 for all of it!

"Thanks for the tips! Just came from jewel and sure enough purchased 14 hunts puddings for 14 bucks and got a $10 cat back! You have turned me into such a great shopper now! And my wife just thinks that adds to my "hotness." ha ha ha.
Thanks again Kimberly."
Mike F.

"Hi Kimberly! Thank you for everything you do! You are such an amazing person. I feel blessed to know you!"
Amanda P.

"I just want to say I really enjoyed your class last week. You have so much information and you seem to genuinely help the rest of us GET IT. Thank you so much. I so want to figure this out. Thank you for giving of yourself, not only to the people you teach, but to the organizations you donate food and necessities to. I just really admire you for what you are doing. "
Dana B.

"I just can't thank you enough for your willingness to share what you have learned with others. I don't know what you'll think of this, but I wanted to tell you that you have been an answer to my prayers. I had been praying for God to help us financially because things have been so tight, and with your help I have been able to provide for my family, and save so much money already."
Marie O.

"The biggest adventure you can ever take is to live the life of your dreams."
Oprah Winfrey

A New Freezer with Free Food, Too!

As I was writing my book, we were faced with scorching temperatures, but I found the coolest deal ever! I had spent a significant time looking at upright freezers. The one I wanted had a door ajar feature, and a temperature control lockout!

I finally decided exactly which freezer model I wanted, had the money saved to purchase it, and even knew exactly where it was going to be set up! When I received my Sunday inserts, I was incredibly excited to see that my freezer was 20% off bringing my cost to around $450 after taxes!

But, then, I saw a small square in the Jewel ad that had my heart racing! A deal was on! For every $100 worth of gift cards I purchased at Jewel, I'd receive a $20 Catalina, to be used like cash at Jewel, on a subsequent transaction.

Guess what?! Jewel sells Sears cards!!! You heard me right! Jewel has a gift card mall in their store, and almost all the cards were participating in this deal! I bought $400 worth of Sears gift cards, and earned $80 to use at Jewel! I made $80!

I was going to buy my freezer anyway, but when it went on sale, I was thrilled, but to earn $80 to a store I already love was just ice cream on a hot summer day. The amount of money I'll save on groceries because I now have a sizeable freezer will be worth the investment very quickly.

I shared my freezer deal in a weekly column I wrote for The Pantagraph, and received the following email in response! You have to love the ingenuity in this deal!

"I was telling my daughter about your recent deal with Jewel gift cards and combining it with your Sears freezer purchase. My son in law must have overheard me because he went and did his own deal. He went to Jewel and bought $300 in Best Buy gift cards and received $60 in coupons for food. Then he went to Best Buy and bought the advertised Play Station 3 for $300. Best Buy then gave him a $100 Best Buy gift card. So for $300 he got his play station 3, a $100 Best Buy gift card and $60 in coupons for Jewel food. This is not bad for his first taste of coupons and refunding!
I enjoy reading your weekly articles. I hope to attend one of your workshops this summer. Thanks for sharing your stories."
Donna D.

Thank You Mom & Dad

On Saturday, March 12, 2011, I lost my dad to pancreatic cancer. He lived in New Mexico, and I was blessed with visits almost every month since his diagnosis in September, 2010.

My dad and I were always close, and I was grateful I didn't have to make up for lost time. The time we had was wonderful, and only re-affirmed how fantastic of a dad he truly was. He was also an amazing writer and poet, and an awesome, awesome grandpa. He was only 64 years old, though, and I thought I would have him in my life for many more years than he was given.

My mama lived about ten minutes from me. My mama was a wonderful mom, always forgiving, always willing to help out, and was always happy to see me, and her grandchildren. She was generous and loving and genuine. She was an amazing artist, with incredible talent, and she shared that creativity as a teacher, art exhibitor, and volunteer.

I was in New Mexico the weekend my dad died, and I was anxious to reach my mama to tell her of the news. I wasn't sure how she would react, and I was concerned. Although my parents were divorced, they were still friends, very much respected one another, and did their best to look out for each other.

When I couldn't reach my mama, I called a good friend of mine and asked her to go to my mom's house to ensure she was alright. I had the opportunity to talk with my mom that Sunday afternoon, and she sounded really good. I can't express the amount of relief I felt when I heard her voice. She told me she missed me, and I told her I loved her, and would be at her house as soon as I got off the plane the following day. And, I was. The moment my plane landed Monday, my husband picked me up and took me directly to my mama's house. It was there that I found my mom on the floor, unresponsive. She spent eight days in ICU, but she never woke up. She died Monday, March 21, 2011. She was also only 64.

With shock and disbelief, I lost both of my parents only nine days apart. The last few months have been difficult, surreal, sad, and the harsh reality is only beginning to settle upon me. However, my parents were absolutely amazing people. They allowed me to be me, and whenever I made a mistake (which was often!), they helped pick me up and encouraged me to move forward.

I've always been involved in social causes, and my parents always supported my ambitions of helping others. I'm who I am today because of my mom and dad, and I'm incredibly blessed to call them my parents.

Your Life is Now

It's never about how much money we have to give, or how much "stuff" we can share with others. It's how much heart we put into giving back. Whether it's coupons, clothing, food, or our time, sharing ourselves with others, to uplift and inspire, is incredibly important, and I ask you to please join the journey I embrace so passionately.

Let us donate, and volunteer, and share our love with our community. Let's have faith, and strong beliefs, and stand up for right and wrong. Let's help those who need us, even if we aren't sure they are ready to accept, and let us go to sleep every night grateful for the opportunities and experiences we've been able to participate in. And, mostly, let us be full of wonder and excitement for every day we have, share our love with our family and friends we adore, and work towards living a life without regrets.

CPSIA information can be obtained at www.ICGtesting.com
Printed in the USA
244896LV00001BA/7/P